Photo...
Co...

Front cover painting by:
Julie Stooks

*We would like to thank the following for
permission to photograph their stock:*
**Hansards Pet Centre,
Romsey**

Your First
LOVEBIRD

CONTENTS

©1996
by Kingdom
Books
PO7 6AR
ENGLAND

your first lovebird

Kingdom Books is an imprint of T.F.H. Publications   **Printed in England.**

INTRODUCTION

Lovebirds are parrots, members of the family **Psittacidae**. Other members of this family include the well-known African Grey Parrot, Amazon parrots, and the ever-popular Budgerigar. Members of the parrot family have attracted and fascinated humans for many centuries: Alexander the Great brought parrots to Europe in the fourth century BC, and even before then parrots were kept as companions. Yet it was not until the 1800s that any scientific system was applied to the keeping of parrots, so it was only then that they were kept with any measurable degree of success.

We have come a long way in parrot husbandry. Nowadays if a keeper has a sound knowledge of his lovebird's requirements, selects his first bird from hardy, domestically-bred stock, and exercises responsibility and common sense in the general care of his birds, he will enjoy a successful and rewarding hobby.

A pair of Lutino Peach-faced Lovebirds. Lovebirds are devoted couples - hence the name.

This book provides basic information for the first-time keeper of lovebirds. It discusses individual species, their general care and feeding requirements, and what a responsible owner can expect in terms of taming and breeding his animals. However, I should stress that, although lovebirds are commonly kept in the bird hobby (and have been since 1900), and demonstrate general hardiness and adaptability, they are not ideal birds for beginners. Such birds as Zebra Finches and Budgerigars are generally better suited as pets for the first-time bird keeper. Starting the parrot-keeping experience with Budgerigars, you will gain valuable knowledge and hands-on experience without unduly endangering the welfare of your charges.

Above all, we must always remember that we keep birds for their sakes and not ours, and that all the pleasure we derive is the by-product of such care. We ensure our success as avian fanciers by putting the birds' welfare first at all times.

Peach-faced Lovebirds.

SPECIES

Lovebirds, of the genus *Agapornis*, are small, stockily built parrots measuring from 12cm to 17cm, with large bills and square or round tails; they are lively and entertaining birds that usually breed well in captivity. Of course, there are exceptions to these rules. Common to all lovebirds is a base colour of green, although many colour-marking mutations and permutations exist among the species. Lovebirds are native to the African continent, with the exception of the Grey-headed Lovebird, which is native to the island of Madagascar. Generally, lovebirds dwell near the Equator and, with the exception of the forest-dwelling Black-collared Lovebird, the wild birds prefer dry savannah regions.

Lovebirds demonstrate a strong bonding between pairs of the opposite sex - a bond so strong that it is said that if one of a pair dies, the other may also pass away from a broken heart, although this story has not been scientifically verified. Nonetheless, the 'loving' bond demonstrated by lovebirds is undeniable. It is not without reason that the Germans call this bird *unzertrennlichen*; the French, *inseparables*; and English-speaking peoples, lovebirds.

However, lovebirds are not solely 'loving' birds. They tend to be aggressive towards birds other than their mate, even within their own species,

(Left) a Pied Lovebird and *(right)* a Normal Peach-faced Lovebird.

and this quality is especially evident between two birds of the same sex. It is also true that lovebirds tend to be noisy, though less so than many of the other parrot species. Therefore, if you need a quiet bird, a member of another bird family is strongly recommended.

However, these disadvantages are balanced by the generally agreeable temperaments of the lovebirds towards humans, the entertaining behaviour they exhibit, the ease with which many lovebirds breed, the relatively easy availability of several lovebird species, and the indisputably attractive colouration that lovebirds display. So, in the end, if you decide that the lovebird is the bird for you, congratulations on an excellent choice.

Peach-faced Lovebird: The scientific name for this species is *Agapornis roseicollis*; it includes the two subspecies *A r roseicollis* and *A r catumbella*. It lives on the western coast of southern Africa, where it feeds mainly on seeds, berries, and fruits. Its natural breeding period is between February and March, and it is a colony breeder, breeding in flocks in the wild. However, in captivity these birds will breed happily in pairs. In the wild they build nests of small twigs and pieces of bark in niches in cliffs and building recesses, and may also breed communally in the nests of weaver birds. Peach-faced Lovebirds are often recommended to the first-time lovebird keeper because they are relatively hardy, require little in the way of special care, breed happily in captivity, and captive-bred birds are readily available at affordable prices.

(Left) **Lutino Masked Lovebird and** *(right)* **Masked Lovebird.**

Lovebirds with White Orbital Rings: The species *Agapornis personata* includes four subspecies: *A p personata* (Masked Lovebird); *A p fischeri* (Fischer's Lovebird); *A p nigrigenis* (Black-cheeked Lovebird); *A p lilianae* (Nyasa Lovebird).

These four races differ in colouration, size, and range but share common feeding and breeding habits. Their diet is made up of various grass seeds and half-ripe maize, berries, fruits, grains and buds. Generally, these birds breed in the hollows of trees, but some will also build nests in trees and on buildings, as well as taking communal nests of weaver birds. The Masked Lovebird and Fischer's Lovebird are often recommended for new lovebird enthusiasts. The Nyasa Lovebird, however, is not common in the hobby and has proved somewhat difficult to breed, while the Black-cheeked Lovebird is rather rare, and is endangered in its native habitat.

Black-winged Lovebird: The species *Agapornis taranta* includes the two subspecies *A t taranta* and *A t nana*. These birds live at high altitudes in their native Ethiopia, sometimes up to one mile above sea level. They are not friendly to humans and are considered by specialists to be among the most 'primitive' species of lovebirds. Certainly they are not recommended for beginners. These birds feed on seeds, fruits, and berries and are known to enjoy juniper berries and the seeds of particular figs in their native land. Black-winged Lovebirds roost in trees and the females build their nests of twigs, grasses and other materials.

Grey-headed Lovebird: The species *Agapornis cana* includes the two subspecies *A c cana* and *A c ablectanea*. This is the only species of lovebird that does not live on the African continent, being a native of Madagascar. It prefers the open savannah and avoids human settlements. Both races are considered shy birds and, like the Black-winged Lovebird, are among the most primitive of the lovebird species. They, too, are not recommended for beginners. Their primary food is grass seeds, supplemented with grains, rice, and various fruits. In the wild, these birds nest during November and April. Their nests are built of grasses, leaves, and bark and are constructed in tree cavities.

Black-collared Lovebird: The species *Agapornis swinderniana* includes the three subspecies *A s swinderniana*, *A s zenkeri*, and *A s emini*. Black-collared Lovebirds are rarely imported as they are very fussy eaters in the captive state, and many die of starvation. Additionally, they are difficult to breed in captivity, because of their natural inclination to nest in termite mounds; the nests are hollowed out by the females. Their natural breeding season is in July. As can be seen, Black-collared Lovebirds are certainly not for the beginner.

Red-faced Lovebird: The species *Agapornis pullaria* includes the two subspecies *A p pullaria* and *A p ugandae*. Found throughout central Africa, this species has the most extensive range of all the lovebirds. It can be found in either overgrown or semi-open savannah, but tends to avoid

Two beautiful Cremello Lovebirds. (Cremello is a new mutation.)

highland forests. Its feeding habits are similar to those of most of the other species of lovebirds. It eats mainly grass seeds, but also takes berries, fruits and wild figs. The natural breeding season is between October and February. At first glance, it may seem that the Red-faced Lovebird is a good bird for the beginner. However, like the Black-collared Lovebird, it breeds naturally in termite mounds, so it is not recommended for inexperienced fanciers. Additionally, the Red-faced Lovebird is not very adaptable and, like the Grey-headed and Black-winged Lovebirds, is among the primitive species of this genus.

SUMMING UP

From the above, it is clear that there are considerable differences among the various species, with some making good first-time lovebird pets and others being far beyond the abilities of a novice keeper. Undoubtedly, the best species for the new lovebird owner are Peach-faced Lovebirds, Masked Lovebirds, and Fischer's Lovebirds. From now on, I shall discuss the various aspects of lovebird keeping and care with these three species in mind.

A group of Peach-faced Lovebirds enjoying each other's company with a Pied to the far left.

PURCHASE

Now you have decided upon your species of lovebird, the main issues are where to get your bird, what it needs, and how you choose it. This chapter deals with each of these concerns separately.

BREEDER OR PET SHOP?

As said previously, I am assuming that we are dealing with one of the three recommended lovebirds - the Peach-faced, Masked, or Fischer's Lovebirds. These birds are commonly bred in domestic aviaries, both by commercial establishments and by individual fanciers. When you set out to purchase your lovebirds, take your time and look at as many birds as possible.

The best quality birds will be available direct from the breeder. The local bird club should be able to put you in touch with breeders in your area. If you cannot find a local breeder, the next best place is a pet shop specialising in birds. A good pet shop should offer only captive-bred birds. Most captive-bred birds have rings on their legs, telling you the year that they were born. Don't worry too much if the birds are not ringed as lovebirds breed so easily in captivity that it is no longer cost-effective to import them on a large scale. Some older birds may have been imported, but will have adapted to captivity. As a first time owner it is always better to go for a young bird. Do try to visit the pet shop several times before buying your bird. The appearance of the shop should be consistently clean and tidy and the birds well cared for each time you visit.

WHAT DOES THE BIRD NEED?

The new lovebird needs: a suitably-sized cage or aviary equipped with food and water bowls and perches, food (seeds, greenfood, and so on); bird sand, grit, and other such substances; a suitable place to locate the cage; and its owner's earnest desire to provide well for the animal. The cage and its accessories can be purchased at a local pet shop, as can the food and grit. A suitable location and a desire to provide proper care are issues solely in the owner's control and can make all the difference to a lovebird's welfare.

It is very important to be fully prepared before bringing your new lovebird home. This means not only that you have all the necessary equipment ready in the home but also that you and all the members of the household are fully prepared to assume your new responsibility. You should all be aware of the fact that the lovebird is likely to be a member of the family for at least the next seven years. (The oldest recorded age of a lovebird in captivity is 17 years!)

Finally, you must make sure that you are able to keep your birds within the home environment. If you rent your home, make sure your landlord has no objections to the keeping of birds. Many landlords will allow birds but not cats or dogs. You have fewer restrictions if you own your home but, if you intend to keep your birds in an outdoor aviary, your neighbours may not appreciate the screeching noises that lovebirds can make.

A happy group of Pastel-blue Peach-faced Lovebirds.

CHOOSING THE BIRDS

Upon first entering the pet shop or breeders' premises, take a good look around to assess the overall maintenance and cleanliness of the area; it should be immaculate. An insanitary or poorly-kept area invites disease and, even if the birds appear healthy, they may be carriers or have recently caught a disease or infection. Never buy a bird or any of its equipment from a poorly-kept establishment.

Next look over the seller's general stock. At first, keep your distance from the cages or aviaries so that you do not disturb the birds. In this way you can get a good idea of the general nature and behaviour of the stock by observing the actions and interactions of the birds. At this point you are looking for healthy exercise and other activity, enthusiastic feeding, mutual and individual grooming, and proper sleeping positions, depending on the time of day.

Now inspect each of the cages or aviaries individually, carefully assessing the general behaviour and appearance of its occupants. Definite warning signs of unhealthy lovebirds include: lethargy and apathy; discharge from the eyes or nose; discoloured or encrusted feathers around the anus; fluffed plumage; large bald patches and/or skin irritations; laboured or noisy breathing; and roosting on two feet, especially on the ground (birds typically perch high up, on one leg). Do not purchase a bird exhibiting any of these signs or, indeed, any bird from the entire stock - infection and disease can spread very rapidly among our avian friends. At the same time, check for deformities, especially of the bill and feet. While genetic deformities in a given bird may make it an undesirable purchase, these deformities are not transferred to other birds except through breeding. Overgrown bills and claws, on the other hand, are usually the result of improper care and are a strong warning to the potential owner not to purchase any bird from those premises.

Now you can begin to select your individual bird(s). Choose a bird that you feel demonstrates the best signs of health and quality. Don't be sentimental and choose a bird that seems 'in need of a good home', as you are likely to end up with one that soon dies.

When you have selected a lovebird, ask the proprietor to handle the bird so that you can inspect it closely. Handling inflicts considerable stress on the animal, and some birds have been known to suffer heart failure as a result. For this reason, insist that the seller handles the bird, and at the same time you can see how experienced he or she is.

Once the bird settles in the seller's control, closely inspect its eyes, feathers, anal vent, and other points already discussed. Additionally, check its breast with your fingers. If the bird lacks substance to its breast, it is likely to be suffering from some form of nutritional deficiency and is best not purchased. If the bird passes the inspection to your satisfaction, question the seller about the bird to assure yourself of its health and proper care, as well as to become aware of any peculiarities that it might have exhibited in terms of feeding, fighting, and other behaviour.

When you buy the bird, insist on some form of written guarantee that allows you to return the animal within a few days if it does not pass the inspection of the veterinary surgeon of your choice.

If you choose to keep a pair of lovebirds rather than a single pet and the seller has already paired his animals your job is made considerably easier. In fact, I recommend that as a first-time buyer you purchase only 'guaranteed' pairs, if a pair is what you want. It is particularly difficult for novice fanciers to sex birds, especially when the birds are young. Even if the birds are correctly sexed but have not yet demonstrated compatibility, there is no guarantee that they will exist peacefully in the confines of the cage; and there is a very real danger of eventual aggression between two birds of the same sex.

If you want a breeding pair, it is better to purchase only 'proven' pairs, that is, pairs that have already successfully produced and reared offspring. While 'guaranteed' and 'proven' pairs will probably cost more than two singly purchased birds, it is worth it to have a better chance to have compatible and long-lived pets.

TRANSPORT AND QUARANTINE

The journey home can prove lethal if the lovebird is not protected from draughts, panic reactions and undue stress.

Birds are very intolerant of draughty conditions which, even if of short duration, can lead to illness easily. Therefore, the transport cage should be fully enclosed, with small offset slits at the top and on the sides of the cage to allow ventilation. Birds will attempt to fly if startled, so the cage must be small enough to contain them securely. Finally, because all the foreign sights and sounds encountered on the way home will stress the lovebirds, the transport cage should be made of wood.

Ideally, each bird should be given a transport cage of its own. While you can build these cages yourself, it is better to buy purpose-built boxes at a local pet shop or bird-supply warehouse. Purchasing a commercial transport cage is the best way for the new bird owner to ensure the safety of his new pet.

If you already keep other birds in your home, you must quarantine your new lovebird before allowing it near your existing stock. Quarantine means

A young Pastel-blue Peach-faced Lovebird looks around with interest.

that the bird is isolated for a few weeks in a cage of its own, which allows you to monitor it for any signs of a developing illness and other undesirable conditions. Such quarantine is not necessary if your new lovebird is your first bird. However, you should monitor its behaviour and condition closely for the first few weeks. At the first sign of disease, contact your vet.

It is important to remember that the first few weeks in the new home are the most critical for the bird. If it acclimatises successfully to its new home during this crucial period, owner and bird are likely to have a long, healthy and happy relationship.

A pair of Peach-faced Lovebirds enjoying themselves on a nest perch.

A Cremello with two toe-nails missing. This will not affect the bird's ability to grip the perch.

An excited group of Blue Masked Lovebirds with a Normal Masked in the bottom right-hand corner.

KEEPING

Basically there are three different ways of keeping lovebirds in captivity: the cage, the indoor flight, and the outdoor aviary. The vast majority of first-time lovebird keepers house their charges in cages, so these receive the most coverage in this book. You must always make allowances for such factors as flying space, proper food and water receptacles, safe and effective perches, and other accessories.

CAGES

There are two possible ways to keep lovebirds indoors: in a cage or in an indoor flight. From the bird's point of view the indoor flight certainly has advantages over the cage. From the owner's point of view, however, the indoor flight might seem anything but practical.

The indoor cage is by far the most common accommodation for lovebirds. Remember, a large cage is essential for the welfare of your lovebird. One undoubted rule stands: the bigger, the better. Wing flapping and stretching, which often indicate the good health and well-being of your pet, require plenty of space.

The minimum cage size depends upon the number of birds and their relationship to one another. For instance, a mating pair typically requires less space than a pair of individuals, while a single bird will require even less. If you are unsure of the relationship between a number of lovebirds, then the ideal solution could be communal cages, with openings between them for easy passage. Such cages allow the lovebirds to establish their territories and escape aggression if necessary. In terms of the optimum size of single cages, most specialists demand that the cage has minimum dimensions of 80cm x 50cm x 50cm for a pair of lovebirds and 100cm x 100cm x 100cm to house several young birds. You should not keep more than one pair of adult birds in an indoor cage. A rectangular cage is better than a square one of the same area, as the rectangular cage offers your birds more room for flight and other exercise.

Next, examine the construction of the cage. Whether purchased or built, cages must be sturdy, non-toxic, easy to clean and maintain, and offer the birds protection and security. The main frame of the cage, which can be made of wood, metal, or other suitable material, should be free of toxins and other contaminants. Avoid 'pressed' or otherwise-treated woods when choosing cage materials. Your lovebird is sure to put its powerful beak to good use on whatever material you choose! Many specialists recommend that the wood and/or metal is coated with a non-toxic varnish or other finish to make it easier to clean. It is better to avoid using a second-hand cage but, if you must use one, be sure to sterilise it with a disinfectant available at your pet shop or veterinary surgery.

In general, it is preferable if at least two, preferably three, sides of the cage are solid, leaving only the front of the cage composed of wire mesh. This prevents draughts, and gives the birds increased security. If you opt for an all-wire cage, be sure to locate it in a draught-free, quiet (but not uninhabited!) spot in the home; include some type of shelter or 'hiding' place, such as a nesting box, as well. A bright corner of a frequently-occupied room, such as a living room, is ideal for lovebirds as long as the temperature is constant and there are no draughts or excessive noise and excitement. The breeze from a constantly opening and closing door may be a hazard to your lovebird, as would be the ever-changing temperature of a kitchen. The tray at the bottom of the cage should be at least 0.75cm high and slide out for easy cleaning.

Lovebirds love to bathe so equip their cages with a sizable bathing dish in addition to a container for drinking water. You will also need three food trays, which are best attached to the side of the cage and accessible from the outside.

It is important to select natural perches of varying thickness for your lovebirds. Plastic perches can be bad for your birds' feet and give the birds many sleepless nights. Provide several natural branches wide enough for your lovebird to wrap its feet one-half to three-quarters around. As well as being able to flex its feet comfortably, the bird uses the branches to sharpen its beak and claws. Just be sure that the branches are non-poisonous and have not been treated with any chemicals. Place the perches at more than one height to give your birds a variety of sitting positions.

Toys are also a nice inclusion in your lovebird's home. Ladders, mirrors and other toys will inspire your bird to exercise its body and mind, and help to keep it active when alone in its cage. Many experts recommend putting a nesting box inside the cage to give the bird an added sense of security. This is even more essential if the cage is constructed of wire on all sides.

You may believe it is cheaper to construct your lovebird's accommodation yourself. Unless you are a skilled handyman with considerable knowledge of the properties of wood and metal, as well as geometry, what you can make can often be purchased at better quality for less money.

This Lutino seems to be practising a dance step on its perch!

A Pastel-blue Peach-faced Lovebird. Of the many colour mutations of the Peach-faced Lovebird this must be one of the most subtle and attractive.

INDOOR FLIGHTS

An indoor flight is an ideal environment for lovebirds. Flights come in many sizes, but experts recommend a size of 1.6 x 1.6 x 1 metres as sufficient. Take the same care in choosing a location for your flight as you would a cage to ensure the health of your birds. Nesting boxes are more necessary in a flight than a cage, especially if more than one pair of birds is sharing the space. The large size of the flight will give your lovebirds considerable freedom of movement and can, to some degree, simulate their natural environment.

OUTDOOR FLIGHTS

Lovebirds can be kept in outdoor flights as long as certain conditions are met. Principally, outdoor aviaries should be draught-free and dry; they should face the sun and include a shaded, insulated shelter room. Avoid proximity to industrial smoke, busy and noisy traffic, pigeon lofts, other aviaries and poultry farms. Vermin and moist conditions are prevented by a sloping concrete floor and narrow gauge wire mesh but for cost reasons this type of construction is often rejected. Pea shingle, which can be hosed down at regular intervals, and coarse sand, which can be raked clean, are both suitable and more ornamental alternatives to concrete. Rodents can be kept out by burying the mesh down to a depth of 30cm. The mesh around the bottom of the aviary should be fine, or an overlaying double layer can be used. The two layers should stop vermin, cat paws and wild birds from getting in and prevent small birds from getting their heads stuck. Plastic coating on wire mesh is likely to be chewed off. Galvanised wire of the correct gauge (normally 19G) should be used. Cracks and crevices in wooden stakes offer red mites an excellent hiding and breeding environment. Painting with nontoxic paint at regular intervals should destroy such breeding grounds.

Outdoor aviaries should be partly covered by a roof, so that droppings from wild birds, which might contain pathogenic bacteria or parasites, are kept out as much as possible. Covering only half the aviary roof allows the birds to bathe in light showers, but make sure access to shelter is always available in case of heavy rain. Feed and water containers should always be placed in the covered section. Under cold climatic conditions the drinking water could freeze and may be a problem. Change the water frequently, use containers with heating elements or place drinkers in the shelter room.

FEEDING

The importance of correct diet and nutrition cannot be over-emphasised. It contributes significantly to the lovebird's day-to-day health and well-being and its long-term life expectancy. Of course, correct feeding is only a part of the proper care of lovebirds.

Good feeding means providing your lovebirds with the most varied diet possible. In the wild, lovebirds are free to select from a wide assortment of seeds, greens, insects and other foods, so can adjust their diet according to their instincts and needs. As your lovebird's keeper, it is your responsibility to provide this selection as best you can. A rough feeding strategy commonly employed by lovebird keepers is given below.

It begins with a standard seed mixture, which typically includes about ten parts canary seed, three parts brown millet, two parts sunflower seed, one part mixed grass seed, and one-half part hemp seed. Some experts recommend that these seeds are offered in separate containers, perhaps in one of the multi-sectioned food receptacles commonly sold in pet shops. If you do this, you have to buy the seed separately. The argument in favour of offering the seeds in this way is that the keeper can make a better assessment of his birds' intake of each of the various seeds, guarding to some extent against a one-sided intake of only a few seed types.

In the end, most lovebird keepers feed their birds a standard, commercially-prepared mixture specially designed for lovebirds. Each day, you should blow all the empty shells from the bowl, before refilling it with the seed mixture. However, one rule stands firm: no matter how the seeds are presented, they must be supplemented with fruit and greenfood, tree branches, and occasional soft foods.

In addition to seeds, offer a combination of fresh vegetables (greenfood) and/or fruits each day, ideally at least one fruit and one vegetable. One example of this type of food is sprouted seeds. Every lovebird should have sprouted seeds as part of its diet regularly. Sprouted seeds are easily prepared following this recipe: soak the seeds (these may be from the lovebird mix or seeds such as alfalfa) in clean water for 24 hours; rinse the seeds and place them in a warm location for 24–48 hours; when the seeds sprout, rinse them again and feed them to your lovebirds. An important note: seeds that do not sprout in three days are not fresh, and the entire batch should be discarded. Sprouting a sample of seeds is a very common and simple method of testing their freshness.

A colourful mixed group of Peach-faced Lovebirds. The young bird near the back with a 'patchy' appearance is in the process of moulting.

Vegetables can include brussels sprouts, cabbage, spinach and parsley, as well as dandelion, chickweed, shepherd's purse and others. Some common fruits include figs, soaked raisins, apples, sweet oranges, and soft pears and peaches. An excellent food for your lovebirds is half-ripe maize, still on the cob. Maize is fresh only in late summer, but it can easily be frozen for use throughout the winter and early spring. Berries, such as rosehips and rowan berries, can be offered occasionally. Offer the fruits and vegetables in moderation: an excess of these types of foods can lead to digestive problems, first seen in either loose stools or constipation.

Fresh tree branches, especially branches from fruit trees, provide a very important part of the lovebird's diet. In addition to serving as perches and giving the birds an excellent material on which to work their beaks, tree branches provide many necessary vitamins and minerals from the bark, as well as roughage that aids in digestion. Fresh tree branches should always be available to the birds and should be replaced whenever they are stripped of their bark.

You can give a little soft food, such as hard-boiled egg yolk, cooked wheat and other cereals, perhaps on a monthly basis and more frequently during the breeding season. As with fruits and vegetables, an excess of soft foods can lead to digestive problems.

WATER

Provide fresh water daily, in a bowl that allows the lovebird easy access: the lovebird drinks by submerging its lower bill and then lapping up the water by rapidly moving its tongue. Place the water bowl in a shady location in the cage, and wash it thoroughly every day. Although a lovebird will refuse to bathe in dirty water, it will drink it, and the ingestion of stale water can easily lead to disease.

Many people who choose to keep birds do so simply to have a tame pet. Others keep birds for breeding, research, aesthetics, and many other reasons. If you are one of those people who desire a tame companion, select your lovebird from young stock. As a general rule, lovebirds that possess a black colouration to their beak are young birds. It might also be better to keep your lovebird singly and not as one of a pair, for single birds usually become tamer than couples.

After selecting a young bird, the next step involves spending plenty of time with it every day. After the first few days in the new home, when the

A Lutino *(foreground)* and a Masked *(background)*.

bird is more used to you and its surroundings, begin the taming process by talking softly to it; you should do this while you are presenting its food and water or servicing the cage, and as often as you can throughout the day. Keep your movements slow and smooth - avoid jerky, sudden motions that will startle and intimidate the young bird.

Once you feel that your companion is comfortable with you, and you with it, you are ready to take the next step towards hand-taming. Place a dowel against the bird's breast and try to get it to step up onto the dowel. Probably it will take some time, especially with older birds, but encourage your bird with sunflower seeds, millet spray, or other treats.

When your lovebird is stepping onto the dowel without any problems, it is time to teach it to step onto your finger. The training may follow something like this: have the bird step onto the dowel; wait a moment while talking sweetly to the animal and slowly moving your finger to its breast; now, coaxing gently, try to get the bird to step up to your finger. Like the initial dowel exercise, this procedure may take some time. Once finger-tame, your lovebird is probably on its way to becoming a very tame companion. Don't expect too much, however, and appreciate any affection and co-operation given by the bird. Birds, like humans, are individuals, and no-one can guarantee how tame any lovebird will become, however good the intentions and efforts of the trainer.

Although lovebirds are not considered good talkers - at best they may come to know a few words and noises - they can be taught to perform many tricks, such as climbing ladders and ringing bells. The prime requisites for any training are patience and plenty of treats!

Essentially, taming involves conditioning the bird to accept and trust you. In so doing, you are building a relationship with the animal that it may well come to depend upon. If you plan to purchase a young bird, tame it, and keep it singly, you are assuming very considerable responsibility. We know that most lovebirds are bonding animals and, without an avian mate, a lovebird may well select you as its lifelong companion. When this occurs, it is essential that you spend regular periods of time every day with your lovebird. Should you fail to do so, the lovebird will suffer stress and is more likely to succumb to illness.

BREEDING

Many of the new lovebird keepers reading this book will want to breed from their birds and at least will experiment with breeding. However, breeding is

A pair of Pastel-blue Peach-faced Lovebirds.

best left to experienced lovebird keepers. Despite the fact that the common species of lovebirds breed relatively well in captivity and are generally hardy and easy to care for, breeding places considerable demands on both birds and bird keeper. As a first-time keeper you should not include breeding as part of your first-year plans. Rather, you should try to acquire as much knowledge as possible about lovebirds, your particular species of lovebird, and indeed your own stock, before planning a breeding programme.

The keeper who decides to breed his birds must consider the need for the following: a special diet; special accommodation; the possibility of egg binding and other breeding complications, including the need to hand-rear the nestlings; the proper way to conduct nest checks and keep accurate breeding records; likely veterinary costs; and many other factors too numerous to list here.

ILLNESS

Although, once acclimatised, lovebirds are relatively hardy birds, like all other animals they are subject to various diseases and ill conditions. As with other pets, the key to keeping your lovebirds healthy is prevention. Prevention in the case of lovebirds begins with the selection of an appropriate site for the cage, a site that is warm, clean, and draught-free. Prevention includes the selection of an appropriately-sized and constructed cage. Prevention includes proper feeding and daily inspection of the birds for any signs of illness or poor condition.

Part of the difficulty in treating illnesses in birds is that there are few really distinguishing signs, though there are many general symptoms that suggest any number of diseases or conditions. Common tell-tale signs of illness include: watery and/or dull eyes, runny nose, odd breathing of any type, apathy, lethargy, dull plumage, bald patches, refusal to eat and/or drink, and perching at night on two feet, especially on the ground. These are a few of the most commonly-observed signs. By knowing your birds through daily inspection you will notice any changes immediately, preventing something simple from becoming life threatening.

Diseases and illnesses can be caused by genetic, environmental (including feeding), bacterial, viral, or other factors. This is not the place to detail all the many parrot and other bird diseases known, but it is important to make a note of 'parrot fever', also known as psittacosis. At one time this disease ran rampant through the domestic stocks of parrots throughout Europe and other parts of the world. It brought panic, import and export restrictions, and an increased need for quarantine of new birds. Today there is antibiotic treatment for the disease, which must be prescribed by a vet. Because the disease is highly contagious and not limited to parrots - indeed, it can infect man - any outbreak must be reported immediately to the appropriate authorities. Happily, psittacosis is becoming very rare because of captive breeding.

Parasites often plague our pets, and parrots are no exception. External parasites include red mites, mange mites, and lice. If these blood-sucking parasites occur in large enough numbers, they can seriously weaken or even kill the bird. Additionally, these parasites can carry various diseases. As well as inspecting your animals, it is vital that you maintain the utmost cleanliness and hygiene, and routinely treat the bird's living area with a proven, safe pesticide made specifically for birds. Common signs of external parasites include bald patches, irritated skin, and scratching.

Internal parasites include various worm forms such as roundworms, threadworms, and cecal worms. Although internal parasites can be diagnosed by general weakness, weight loss, and loose stools, it is best to have stool examinations performed by a vet, who can then prescribe any necessary treatment.

Feather plucking is a fairly common vice in the parrot world: the bird plucks the feathers from its own body, and sometimes also from its mate's. Possible causes of feather plucking include: nutritional deficiency, stress, poor environmental conditions, disease, and even boredom (especially if the bird has lost a mate or companion). Unless the case is mild and you believe that you know the cause and can treat it, it is best to have a vet or bird specialist take a look at your animal. Treatment will depend on the cause of the condition.

Moulting is not an illness but a natural process by which the plumage is renewed. During the moult, you must keep watch that no irregularities occur, such as gaps in the plumage or the inability to fly. In general, moulting proceeds smoothly, provided that the bird is in fine condition both at the beginning and throughout the process. It is probably a good idea to supplement the bird's diet with vitamin and mineral supplements and/or sprouted seeds and fresh fruits and vegetables to ensure nutritional soundness at this time.

THE WORLD OF LOVEBIRDS
J Brockmann and
W Lantermann
ISBN 0-86622-927-2
H-1092
Every known colour variety of the various lovebird species is given coverage in this masterfully detailed text, with special attention paid to the methods of breeding them successfully.
Hardcover: 150mm x 225mm, 192 pages, 71 full-colour photos

BREEDING LOVEBIRDS
Tony Silva and Barbara Kotlar
ISBN 0-86622-722-9
KW-125
This book presents sensible, easy-to-follow advice about all aspects of caring for and breeding lovebirds.
Hardcover: 135mm x 200mm, 96 pages, illustrated with full-colour and black and white photos

TAMING AND TRAINING LOVEBIRDS
Risa Teitler
ISBN 0-86622-986-8
KW-038
This book presents sensible, easy-to-follow advice on the selection and care of lovebirds, with special reference to taming them.
Hardcover: 135mm x 200mm, completely illustrated with full-colour photos and drawings, 128 pages

THE ATLAS OF PARROTS
Dr David Alderton
H-1109
ISBN 0-86622-120-4
As well as giving details of every species and subspecies of parrot throughout the world, this comprehensive work also gives information about keeping parrots in captivity. Topics include housing, feeding, health concerns and keeping parrots as pets. Lavishly illustrated with full-colour pictures by Graeme Stevenson, this beautiful book will be of interest to anyone with an enthusiasm for parrots.
Hardcover: 250mm x 350mm, 544 pages, illustrated throughout with full-colour drawings and photographs.

THE PROPER CARE OF LOVEBIRDS
Murray Greenleaf
ISBN 0-86622-190-5
TW-109
This clearly-written book provides the reader with all the basics of lovebird ownership. Topics covered include cages and housing, feeding, colour varieties, breeding, health care and taming.
Hardcover: 125mm x 170mm, 256 pages, illustrated throughout with full-colour photos.

USEFUL ADDRESSES

Royal Society for the Prevention of Cruelty to Animals (RSPCA)
The Causeway
Horsham
West Sussex   RH12 1HG
Tel: 01403 264181

National Council for Aviculture
4 Haven Crescent
Werrington
Stoke-on-Trent
Staffs   ST9 0EY